R.E.M.

Play Along with 8 Great-Sounding Tracks

Contents

Alfred Publishing Co., Inc.
16320 Roscoe Blvd., Suite 100
P.O. Box 10003
Van Nuys, CA 91410-0003
alfred.com

ISBN-10: 0-7390-4973-9 (Book & CD)
ISBN-13: 978-0-7390-4973-0 (Book & CD)

CD recorded at the Mews Recording Studios, London
www.themewsrecordingstudios.com
Dave Clarke, recording and mix engineer
Tom Fleming, guitars
Neil Williams, bass
Noam Lederman, drums

Book edited by Lucy Holliday
Music arranged and engraved by Tom Fleming

Cover photo: © David Belisle

BAD DAY

Words and Music by WILLIAM BERRY, PETER BUCK,
MICHAEL MILLS and MICHAEL STIPE

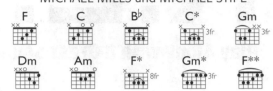

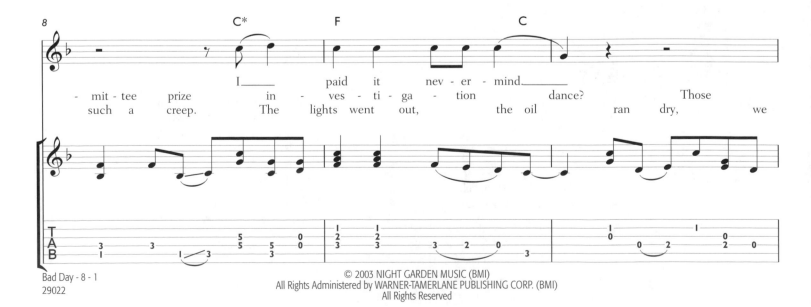

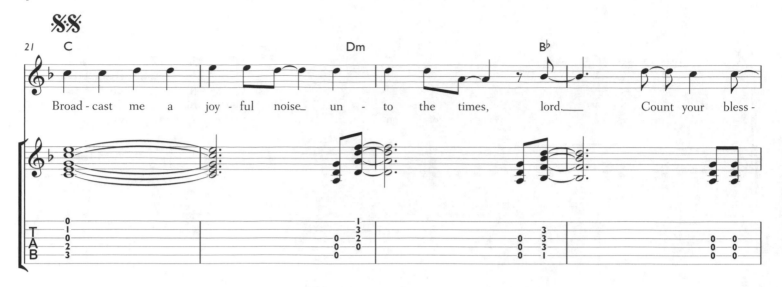

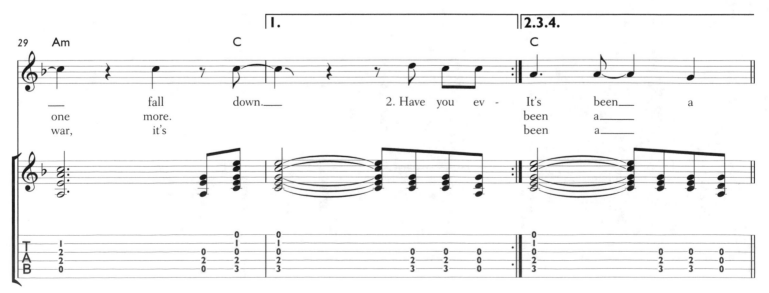

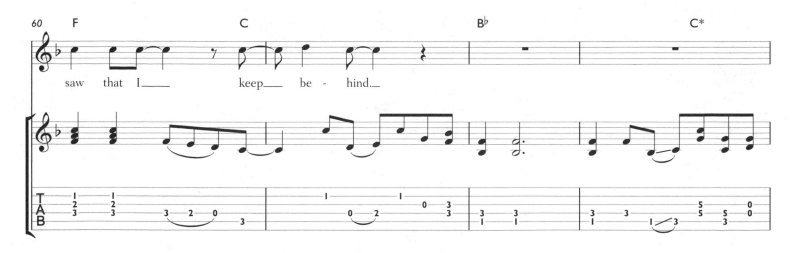

LOSING MY RELIGION

Words and Music by WILLIAM BERRY, PETER BUCK, MICHAEL MILLS and MICHAEL STIPE

MAN ON THE MOON

Words and Music by WILLIAM BERRY, PETER BUCK,
MICHAEL MILLS and MICHAEL STIPE

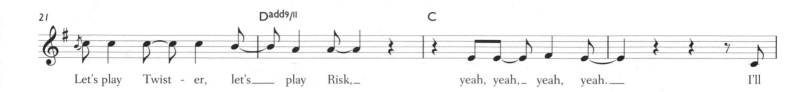

Let's play Twist- er, let's___ play Risk,___ yeah, yeah,_ yeah, yeah.___ I'll

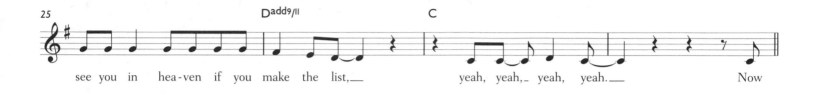

see you in hea-ven if you make the list,___ yeah, yeah,_ yeah, yeah.___ Now

An - dy, did you hear a - bout this one? Tell me, are you locked in the punch?

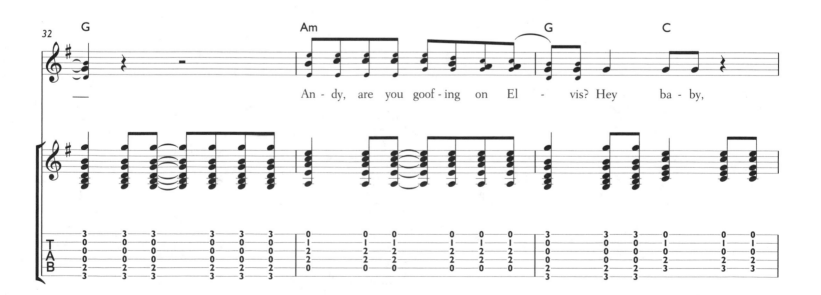

An - dy, are you goof - ing on El - vis? Hey ba - by,

18

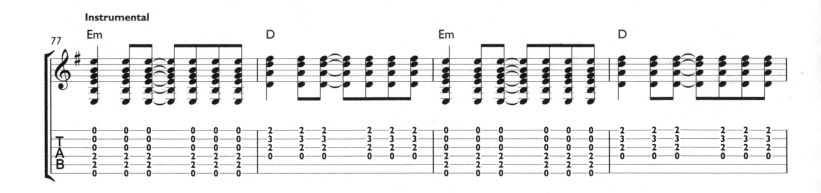

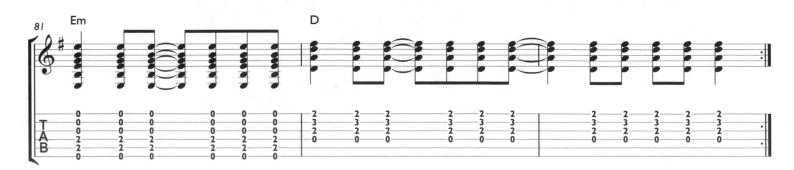

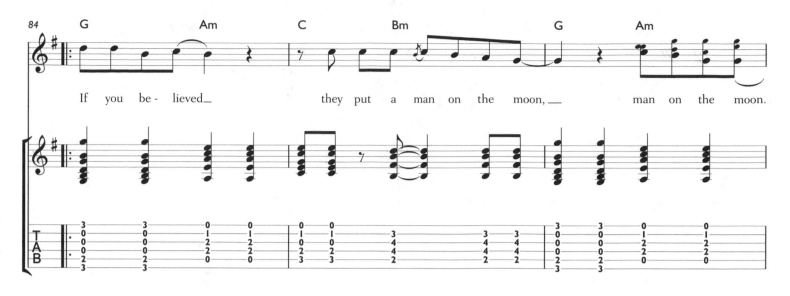

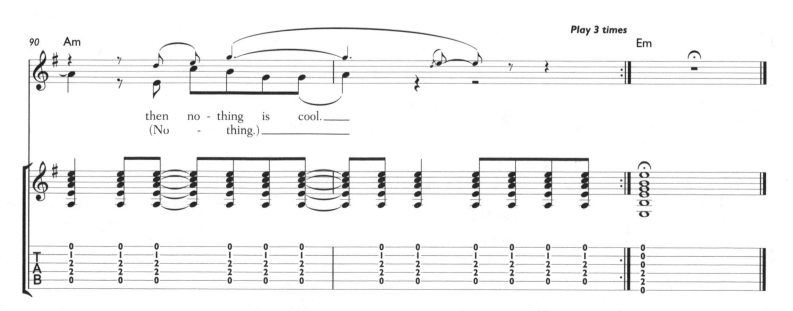

THE ONE I LOVE

Words and Music by WILLIAM BERRY, PETER BUCK,
MICHAEL MILLS and MICHAEL STIPE

17
Em7
Dsus2
Em7
This one goes out to the one I love.
Fi - re,
21
Em7
Dsus2
Em7
fi - re,
1.
25
Em7
Dsus2
Em7
2.
29
Em7
G5
Dsus4
(Solo)
TAB

3. This one goes_ out to the one I love.___

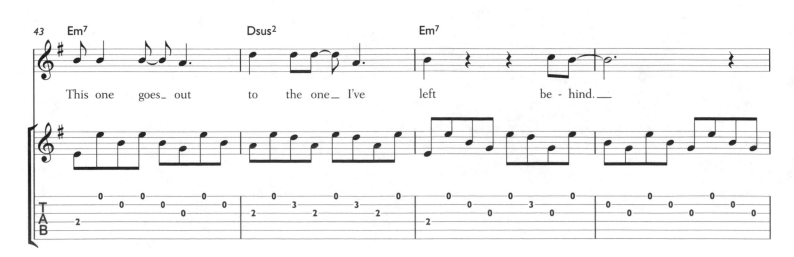

This one goes_ out to the one_ I've left be - hind.___

RADIO FREE EUROPE

Words and Music by WILLIAM BERRY, PETER BUCK,
MICHAEL MILLS and MICHAEL STIPE

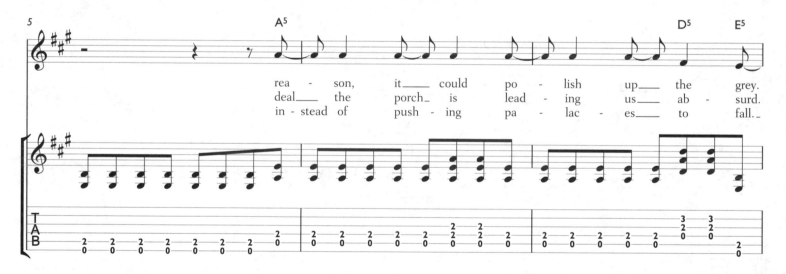

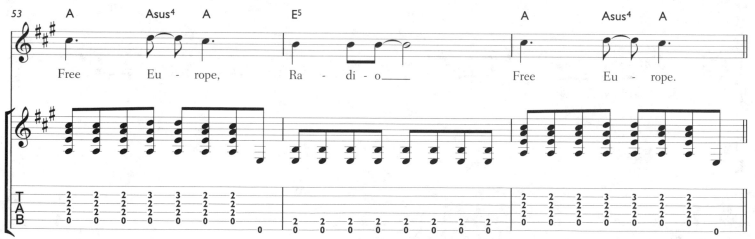

D5 E5 A5
__ that up__ your wall,__ that
__ that to__ the hull,__ that
__ that be - fore all,__ that
- try in__ the wood,__ dis -
D5 E5
__ this is - n't coun - try__ at all.__
__ this is - n't no - thing__ at all.__
this is - n't for - tun - ate__ at all.__
- ap - point__ is in - to us ab - surd.__
F♯7(add11) Aadd9
1,3. Ra - - - - di - - - - o sta - - - - tion,
2,4. Straight off the boat,__

SO. CENTRAL RAIN

Words and Music by WILLIAM BERRY, PETER BUCK,
MICHAEL MILLS and MICHAEL STIPE

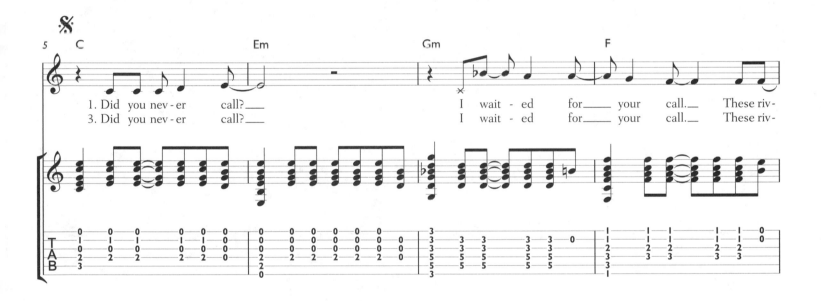

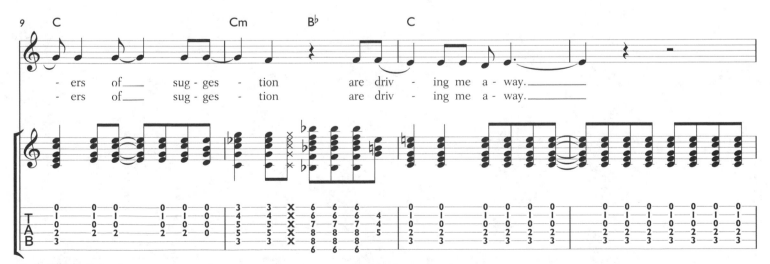

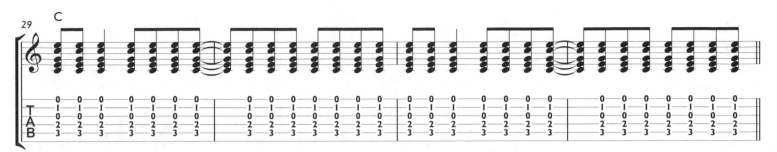

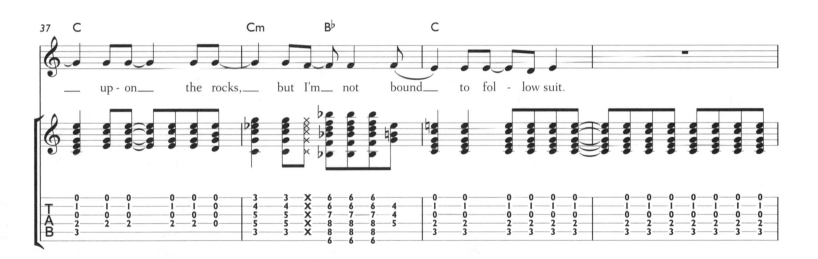

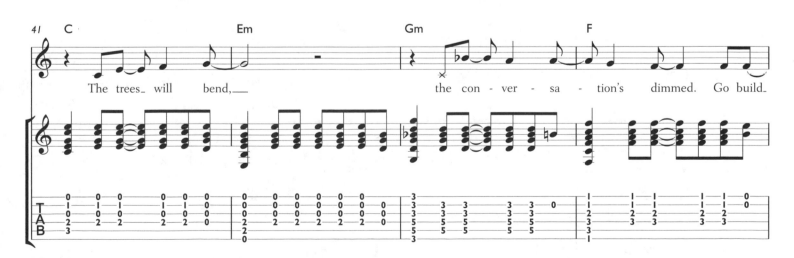

So. Central Rain - 5 - 3
29022

your - self___ an - oth - er home, this choice___ is - n't mine.___

I'm sor - ry,___ I'm sor - ry.___

STAND

Words and Music by WILLIAM BERRY, PETER BUCK,
MICHAEL MILLS and MICHAEL STIPE

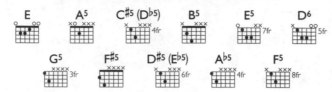

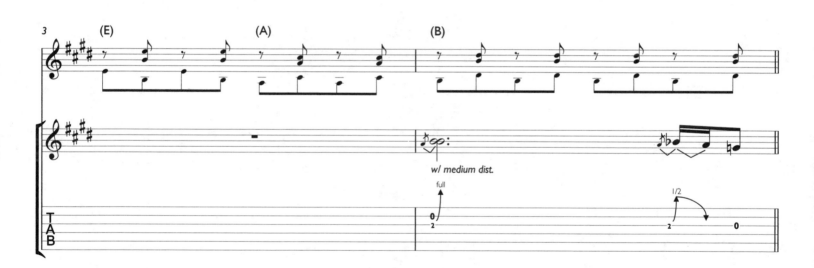

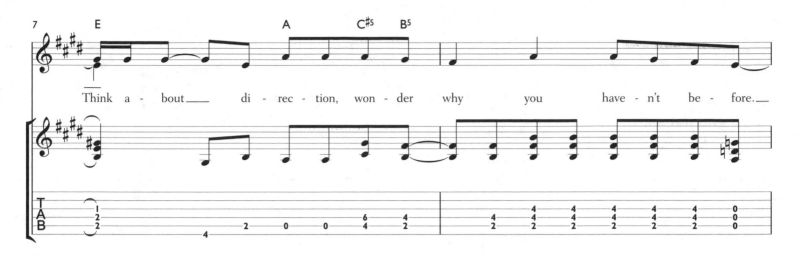

Think a - bout____ di - rec - tion, won - der why you have - n't be - fore.____

Stand in the place where you work,____ now____ face West.____

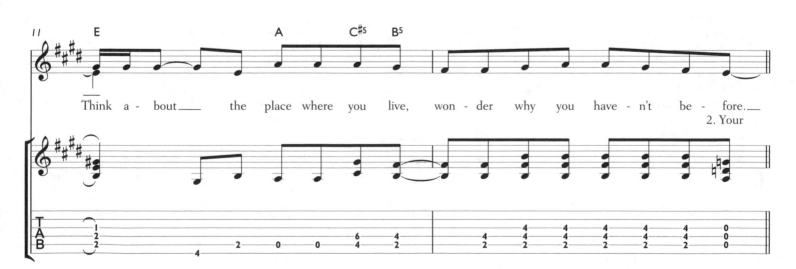

Think a - bout____ the place where you live, won - der why you have - n't be - fore.____

2. Your

Stand - 7 - 2
29022

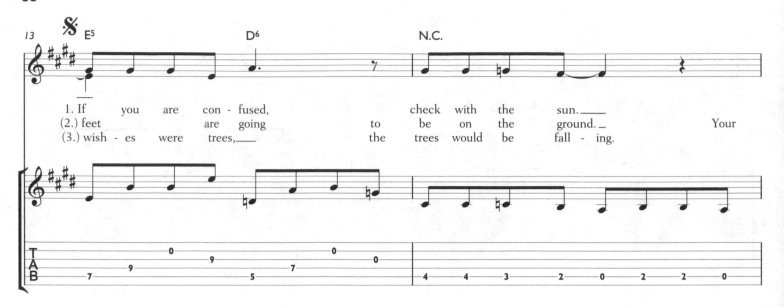

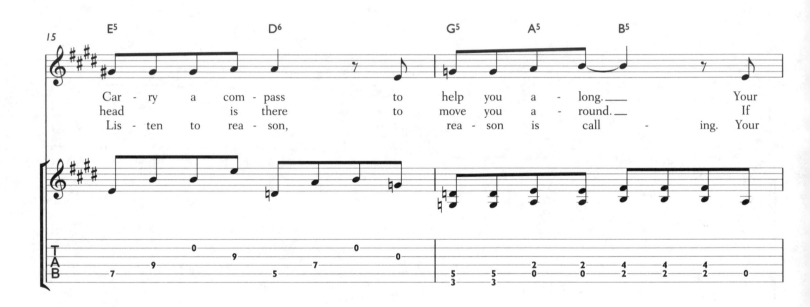

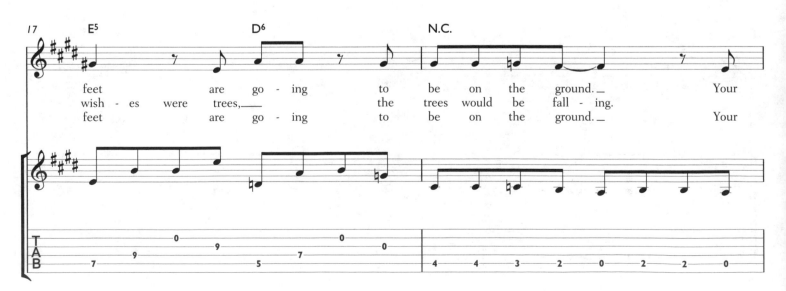

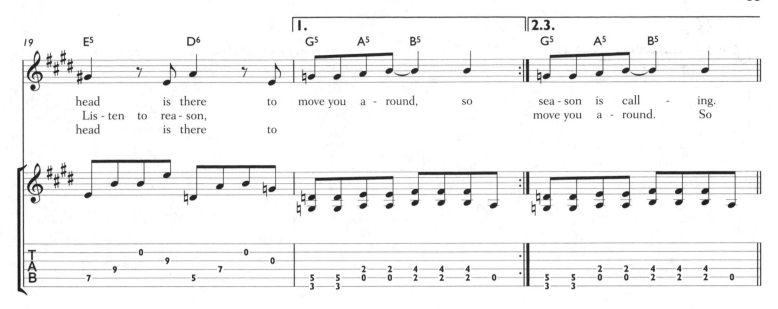

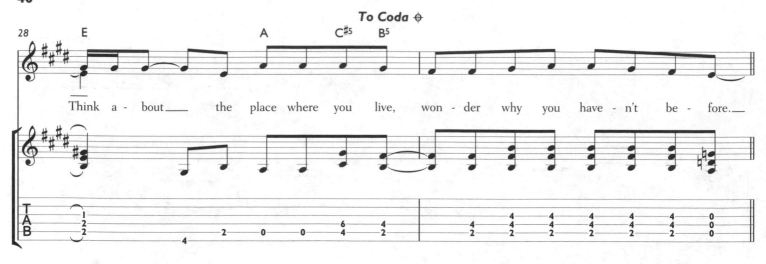

Think a-bout___ the place where you live, won-der why you have-n't be-fore.___

(Solo)
w/ auto-wah effect

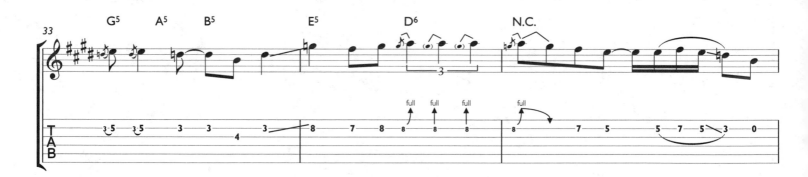

3. If

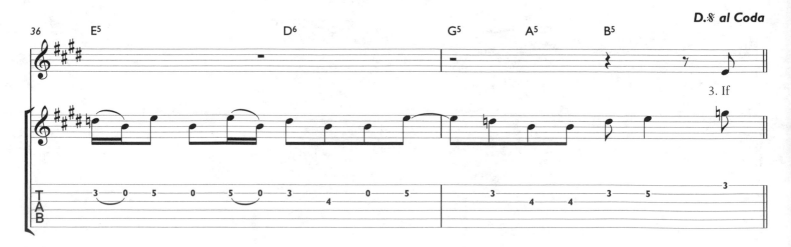

WHAT'S THE FREQUENCY, KENNETH?

Words and Music by WILLIAM BERRY, PETER BUCK,
MICHAEL MILLS and MICHAEL STIPE

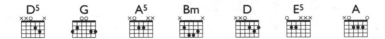

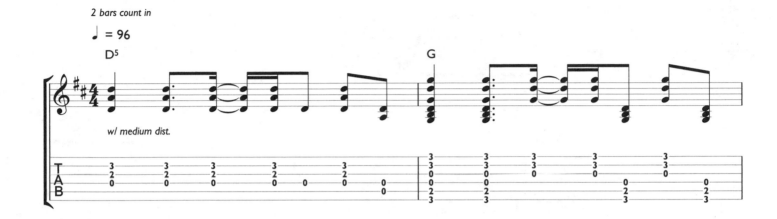

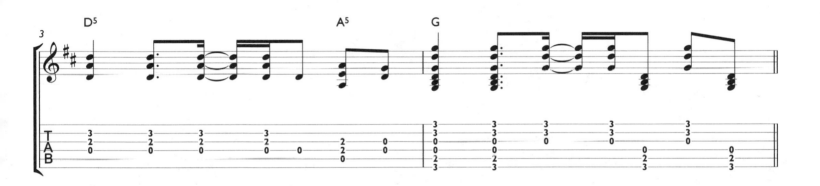

1. "What's the fre-quen-cy, Ken - neth?" is your Ben - ze - drine,__ uh - huh.
2. I'd stu - died your car - toons, radi - o, mu - sic, T. V.,__ movies, maga - zines.
3. (%) "What's the fre-quen-cy, Ken - neth?" is your Ben - ze - drine,__ uh - huh.

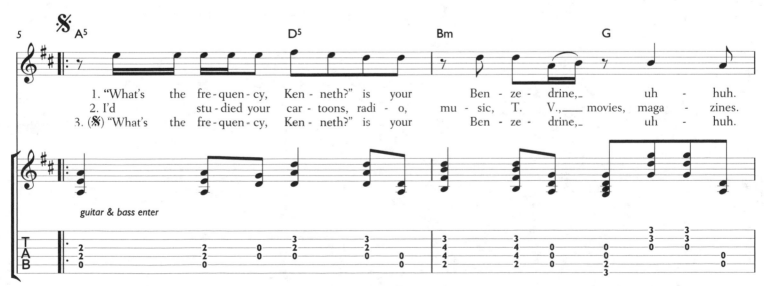

What's the Frequency, Kenneth? - 5 - 1
29022

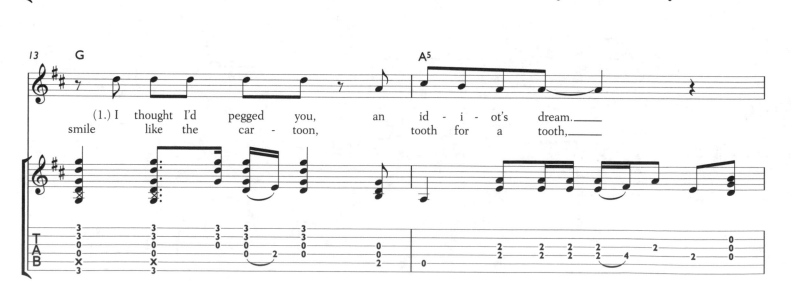

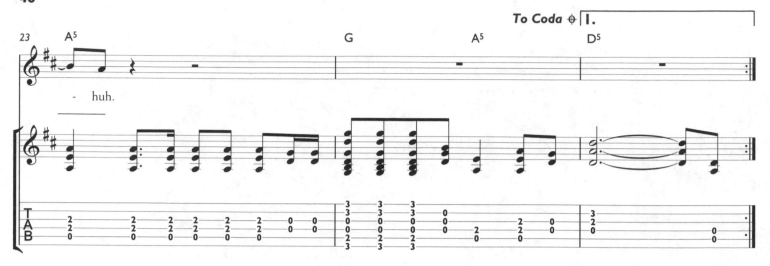

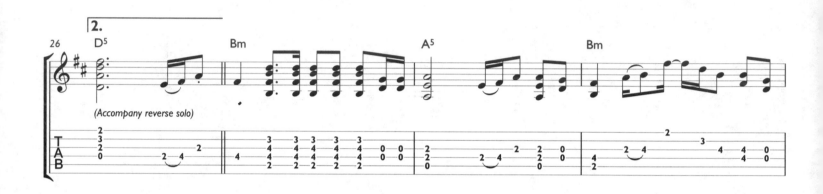

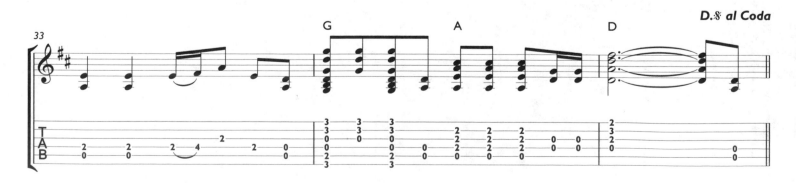

Guitar TAB Guide

Understanding Chord Boxes
Chord boxes show the neck of your guitar as if viewed head on—the vertical lines represent the strings (low E to high E, from left to right), and the horizontal lines represent the frets.

An X above a string means "don't play this string."

An O above a string means "play this open string."

The black dots show you where to put your fingers.

A curved line joining two dots on the fretboard represents a "barre." This means that you flatten one of your fingers (usually the first) so that you hold down all the strings between the two dots at the fret marked.

A fret marking at the side of the chord box shows you where chords that are played higher up the neck are located.

Tuning Your Guitar
The best way to tune your guitar is to use an electronic tuner. Alternatively, you can use relative tuning; this will ensure that your guitar is in tune with itself but won't guarantee that you will be in tune with the original track (or other musicians).

How to Use Relative Tuning
Fret the low E string at the 5th fret and pick the note; compare this with the sound of the open A string. The two notes should be in tune. If not, adjust the tuning of the A string until the two notes match.

Repeat this process for the other strings according to the diagram on the right:

Note that the B string should match the note at the 4th fret of the G string, whereas all the other strings match the note at the 5th fret of the string below.

As a final check, ensure that the bottom E string and top E string are in tune with each other.

5th fret

Detuning and Capo Use
If the song uses an unconventional tuning, it will say so clearly at the top of the music (for example, "6 = D" [tune the sixth string to D]) or "tune down a whole step." If a capo is used, it will tell you the fret number to which it must be attached. The standard notation will always be in the key at which the song sounds, but the guitar TAB will take tuning changes into account. Just detune/add the capo and follow the fret numbers. The chord symbols will show the sounding chord above and the chord you actually play below in brackets.

Use of Figures
Figures that occur several times in a song will be numbered (e.g., "Fig. 1," "Fig. 2," etc.) A dotted line underneath shows the extent of the "figure." When a phrase is to be played, it will be marked clearly in the score, along with the instrument that should play it.

Reading Guitar Tablature (TAB)
Guitar tablature, or TAB, illustrates the six strings of the guitar graphically, showing you where to put your fingers for each note or chord. TAB is usually shown with standard musical notation above it. The guitar TAB staff has six lines, each of them representing a different string. The top line is the high E string, the second line is the B string, and so on. Instead of using note heads, TAB uses numbers which show the fret number to be played by the left hand. The rhythm is indicated underneath the TAB staff. Ex. 1 (below) shows four examples of single notes.

Ex. 2 shows four different chords. The 3rd one (Asus4) should be played as a barre chord at the 5th fret. For the 4th chord (C9), you have to mute the string marked with an "x" (the A string, in this case) with a finger of your fretting hand in order to obtain the correct voicing.

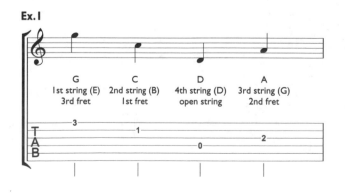

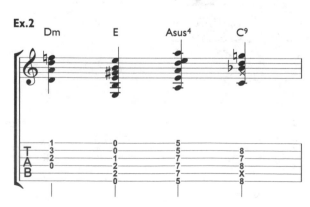

Picking Hand Techniques

1. Down and Up Strokes
These symbols [⊓v] show that some notes are to be played with a down stroke of the pick and others with up strokes.

2. Palm Mute
"P.M." indicates that you need to mute the notes with the palm of the picking hand by lightly touching the strings near the bridge.

3. Pick Rake
Drag the pick across the indicated strings with a single sweep. The extra pressure will often mute the notes slightly and accentuate the final note.

4. Arpeggiated Chords
Strum across the indicated strings in the direction of the arrow head of the wavy line.

5. Tremolo Picking
Tremolo picking is shown by the slashes on the stem of the note. This is a very fast alternate picking technique. Rapidly and continuously move the pick up and down on each note.

6. Pick Scrape
Drag the edge of the pick up or down the lower strings to create a scraping sound.

7. Right Hand Tapping
"Tap" onto the note indicated by a + with a finger of the picking hand. It is nearly always followed by a pull-off to sound the note fretted below.

8. Tap Slide
The tapped note is slid randomly up the fretboard, then pulled off to the following note.

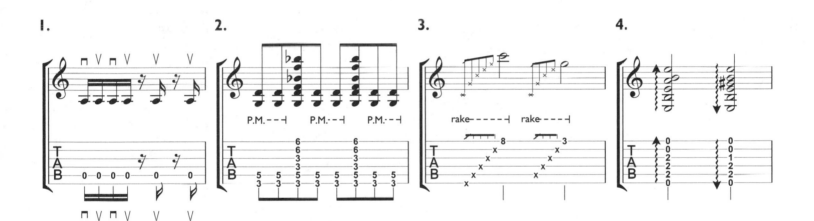

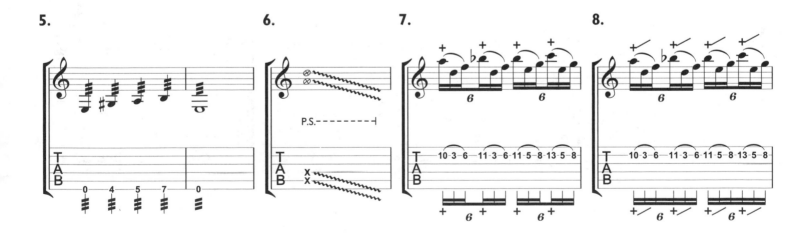

Fretting Hand Techniques

1. Hammer-on and Pull-off
These consist of two or more notes linked together by a slur. For hammer-ons, fret and play the lower note, then "hammer on" to the higher note with another finger. For a pull-off, play the higher note, then "pull off" to a lower note fretted with another finger. In both cases, only pick the first note.

2. Glissandi (Slides)
Fret and pick the first note, then slide the finger up to the second note. If they are slurred together, do not re-pick the second note.

3. Slow Glissando
Play the note(s) and slowly slide the finger(s) in the direction of the diagonal line(s).

4. Quick Glissando
Play the note(s) and immediately slide the finger(s) in the direction of the diagonal line(s).

5. Trills
Play the note and rapidly alternate between this note and the nearest one above in the key. If a note in brackets is shown before, begin with this note.

6. Fret-Hand Muting
Mute the notes with "X" with the fretting hand.

7. Left-Hand Tapping
Sound the note by tapping or hammering on to the note indicated by a [∘] with a finger of the fretting hand.

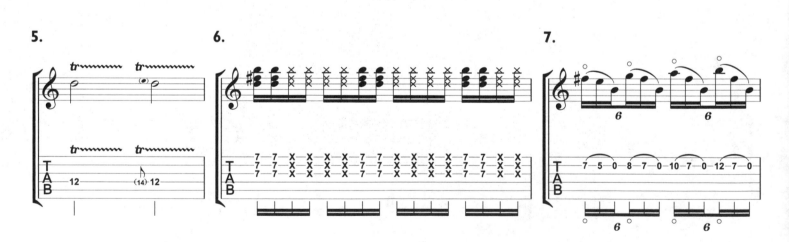

Bends and Vibrato

Bends

Bends are shown by the curved arrow pointing to a number (in the TAB).
Fret the first note and then bend the string up by the value of steps shown.

1. Half-Step Bend
The smallest conventional interval; equivalent to raising the note by one fret.

2. Whole-Step Bend
Equivalent to two frets.

3. Whole-Step-and-a-Half Bend
Equivalent to three frets.

4. Quarter-Step Bend
Bend by a slight degree, roughly equivalent to half a fret.

5. Bend and Release
Fret and pick the first note. Bend up for the length of the note shown. Follow with a release of the bend—letting the string fall back down to the original pitch.

6. Ghost Bend (Pre Bend)
Fret the bracketed note and bend quickly before picking the note.

7. Reverse Bend
Fret the bracketed note and bend quickly before picking the note, immediately let it fall back to the original.

8. Multiple Bends
A series of bends and releases joined together. Only pick the first note.

9. Unison Bend
Strike two indicated notes simultaneously and immediately bend the lower string up to the same pitch as the higher one.

10. Double-Note Bend
Play both notes and bend simultaneously by the value shown.

11. Bend Involving More Than One Note
Bend first note and hold the bend while striking a note on another string,

12. Bend Involving Stationary Notes
Play notes and bend lower string. Hold until release is indicated.

13. Vibrato
Shown by a wavy line. The fretting hand creates a vibrato effect using small, rapid up-and-down bends.

14. Bend and Tap Technique
Play and bend notes as shown, then sound the final pitch by tapping onto note as indicated (by + symbol).

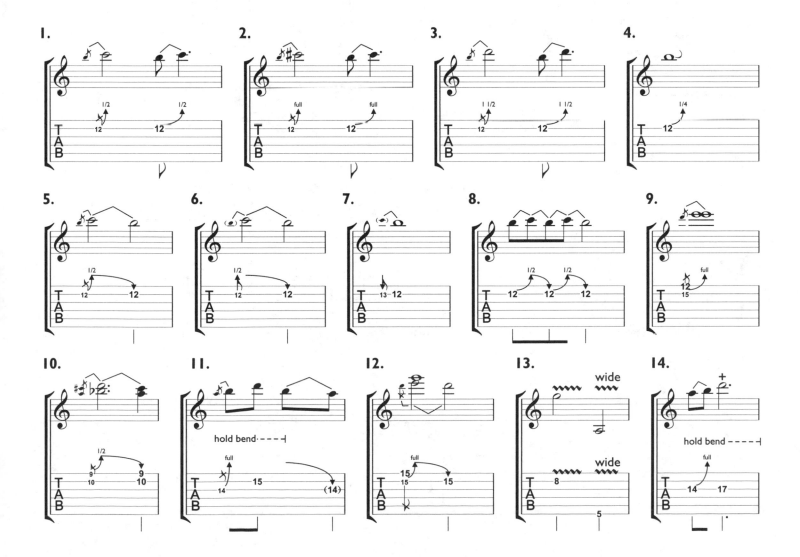

Tremolo Arm (Whammy Bar)

1. Vibrato with Tremolo Arm
Create vibrato using small, rapid inflections of the tremolo arm.

2. Tremolo Arm Dive and Return
Play note and depress tremolo arm by degree shown. Release arm to return to original note.

3. Tremolo Arm Scoop
Depress the arm just before picking the note and release.

4. Tremolo Arm Dip
Pick the note, then lower the arm and quickly release.

5. Sustained Note and Dive Bomb
Play the note, hold for length of time shown and then depress arm to lower the pitch until the strings go slack.

6. Flutter
Pick the note and flick the tremolo arm rapidly with the same hand, making the pitch quiver.

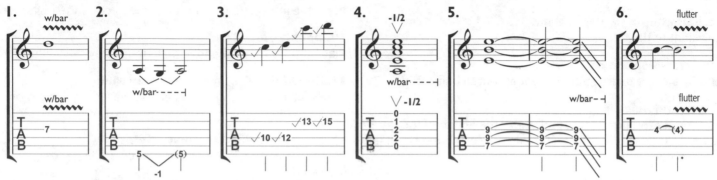

Harmonics and Other Techniques

1. Natural Harmonics
Instead of fretting normally, touch the string lightly with the fretting hand at the fret shown in the TAB. Pick as normal. Diamond noteheads show the resultant pitch.

2. Artificial Harmonics
The first TAB number is fretted and held with the fretting hand as normal. The picking hand then produces a harmonic by using a finger to touch the string lightly at the fret shown by the bracketed number. Pick with another finger of the picking hand.

3. Pinched Harmonics
Fret the note as shown, then create a harmonic by digging into the string with the side of the thumb as you pick.

4. Tapped Harmonics
Fret the note as shown, then create a harmonic by tapping lightly with the picking hand at the fret shown in brackets.

5. Touch Harmonics
Fret the first note, hold it, then touch the string lightly at the fret shown at the end of the slur with the picking hand.

6. Violining
Turn the volume control to zero, pick the notes and then turn the control to fade the note in slowly.

7. Left-Hand Fingering
Small numbers show the finger with which each note is to be fretted.

8. Fingerpicking Notation (PIMA)
Notation that shows which finger should be used to pick each note when playing fingerstyle: p = thumb, i = index, m = middle, a = ring.

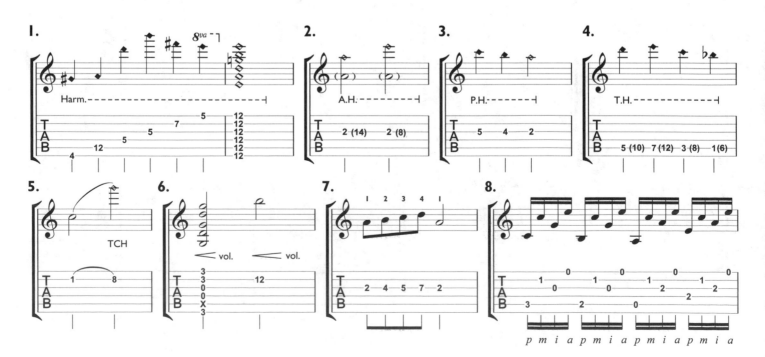